Electronic monitoring in practice: the second year of the trials of curfew orders

by Ed Mortimer and Chris May

A Research and Statistics Directorate Report

Home Office
Research and
Statistics
Directorate

London: Home Office

Home Office Research Studies

The Home Office Research Studies are reports on research undertaken by or on behalf of the Home Office. They cover the range of subjects for which the Home Secretary has responsibility. Titles in the series are listed at the back of this report (copies are available from the address on the back cover). Other publications produced by the Research and Statistics Directorate include Research Findings, the Research Bulletin, Statistical Bulletins and Statistical Papers.

The Research and Statistics Directorate

The Directorate consists of three Units which deal with research and statistics on Crime and Criminal Justice, Offenders and Corrections, Immigration and General Matters; the Programme Development Unit; the Economics Unit; and the Operational Research Unit.

The Research and Statistics Directorate is an integral part of the Home Office, serving the Ministers and the department itself, its services, Parliament and the public through research, development and statistics. Information and knowledge from these sources informs policy development and the management of programmes; their dissemination improves wider public understanding of matters of Home Office concern.

First published 1997

Application for reproduction should be made to the Information and Publications Group, Room 201, Home Office, 50 Queen Anne's Gate, London SW1H 9AT.

©Crown copyright 1996 ISBN 1 85893 997 6
ISSN 0072 6435

Acknowledgements

A great many people in each of the three trial areas assisted with the production of this report. Staff and sentencers in magistrates' courts co-operated fully with the research and tried wherever possible to accommodate the very tight timescales of the research. We would particularly like to thank the following for their help with the sentencing choices survey and analysis of court records: Judith Burrows, David Carrier, Philip Cuddy, Simon Dodgson, Lesley Gilmore, Winston Gordon, Jim Haydock, Kathleen Johnson, Ian Lomax, Katharine Marshall, Stephen Platt, David Ratcliffe, Chris Roberts, John Robinson, Martin Sale, David Scanlan, Liz Wilson and Fiona Young.

We would also like to thank the contractors, Geografix and Securicor Custodial Services, for continuing to give so generously of their time in meeting our requests for information. Particular thanks go to Andy Homer, Paul Reed and Charles Rose of Geografix, and to Ron Robson, Ron Astles, Andrew Davies and Patricia Walmsley of Securicor.

Several staff at the Home Office also worked on various aspects of the report. Colleagues in the Probation Unit provided support and comments on various aspects of the report, especially Allison Harding, Hugh Marriage and Andrew Cunningham.

Within the Research and Statistics Directorate, we would like to thank: Carol Hedderman, Julie Vennard and Chris Lewis for their helpful comments and advice on the various drafts of the report; James Dunmore for advice on the costs model; Joanne Goodman and James Singer for the work on the Offenders Index; Margaret Ayres for providing court data; Andy James for desk-top publishing the report; Eulalia Pereira and Natasha Garnham for their help with the fieldwork; and particularly Darren Sugg, who assisted with data collection, coding and analysis. Finally we would like to thank Professor George Mair of Liverpool John Moores University for providing the independent peer review for this report.

Foreword

Trials of curfew orders with electronic monitoring began in July 1995 in three areas: Greater Manchester, Norfolk and Berkshire. The first twelve months of these trials were evaluated in Home Office Research Study No.163.

This report evaluates the second year of the trials, covering the period July 1996 to June 1997. It examines the rate of use of the order over this period; the characteristics and offending backgrounds of those sentenced; and the immediate outcomes of curfew orders made. There is an analysis of the market share of electronic monitoring to identify which sentences it is competing with, and a model of the estimated costs for a national roll-out of the sentence.

As in the first year of the trials, the results are generally positive. The number of offenders tagged rose significantly as new courts were brought into the trials and as sentencers grew more accustomed to the availability of curfew orders, and the completion rate remained high. Despite these successes, the curfew order with electronic monitoring remains an infrequently used disposal compared to other community sentences. The analysis suggests that the cost per order is comparable to other community sentences, and that if sufficient offenders were tagged rather than sent to prison, the use of electronic monitoring could generate significant savings.

CHRIS LEWIS

Head of Offenders and Corrections Unit,
Research and Statistics Directorate

Contents

Summary

The current trials of curfew orders with electronic monitoring

The curfew order with electronic monitoring was introduced as a sentence in its own right in the 1991 Criminal Justice Act and, following an amendment in the 1994 Criminal Justice and Public Order Act it was introduced on a trial basis in Manchester, Norfolk and Reading, starting in July 1995. Take-up was slow for several months. Nevertheless, the trials were extended and the geographical coverage expanded to cover the whole of the counties of Greater Manchester and Berkshire.

By the end of June 1996, a total of 83 offenders had been tagged, and the evaluation of the first year concluded that the equipment worked reliably and that, despite their early reluctance to use the order, sentencers were pleased with the quick detection of violations and the enforcement action that followed (Mair and Mortimer, 1996, p.27).

This report describes results from the second year of the trial. In addition to providing general information about the rate at which different courts were using the new order, the characteristics of those tagged, and completion rates, it examines two important questions:

- which sorts of sentences curfew orders were competing with (the "market share")

- how much a national roll-out of electronic monitoring would cost.

The use of curfew orders

More courts were brought on stream early in the second year of the trials and, together with the growing acceptance of the order by sentencers, probation staff and other agencies, this led to greatly increased use of the order. During the second year of the trials, 375 curfew orders with electronic monitoring were made in the three areas, more than four times as many as in the first year. However, compared to other disposals, the curfew order remained a rarely used sentence. While there were over 300 curfew orders imposed at the adult magistrates' courts, this compared with 2,900 probation orders, 2,400 community service orders, 900 combination orders and 2,800 custodial sentences.[1]

Of the 375 orders in the second year, over two-thirds were made in Greater Manchester, just under a quarter in Norfolk, and the remainder in Berkshire. When court workload was taken into account however, the difference between Norfolk and Greater Manchester was negligible at 13 and 14 per 1,000 cases respectively. In Berkshire, the rate was seven per 1,000 cases.

Who was tagged?

The offences which most commonly resulted in curfew orders were the same as for the first year of the trials: 28 per cent of orders were for theft and handling, 19 per cent for burglary and 13 per cent for driving whilst disqualified. Other offences included taking without consent, causing actual bodily harm, driving with excess alcohol, criminal damage, public order offences, assault of a police constable, drugs offences, indecent assault and arson.

Of the 375 offenders sentenced to curfew orders in this study, 45 (12%) had no previous convictions, though two (1%) had more than 40 and a further 30 offenders (8%) had at least 20 previous convictions. Just under half of the offenders tagged had previous experience of custody, while three-quarters had received a community sentence, two-thirds a financial penalty and three in five had been made the subject of an absolute or conditional discharge.

Completion rates

Eighty-two per cent of those orders imposed during the second year which had come to an end by the time of writing (October 1997) were successfully completed, with 18 per cent being revoked and resentenced. This is an improvement on the completion rate in the first year (75%). It is also equivalent to the rate for probation orders and better than that for community service (71%). The completion rate is especially high in Norfolk, where 93 per cent of offenders finished their orders.

---

1   Home Office Crime and Criminal Justice Unit figures for the same courts. Note that the data for curfew orders with electronic monitoring relate to the period July 1996 to June 1997, while the data for other disposals are from January to December 1996. All of these figures have been rounded to the nearest hundred.

Market share of curfew orders with electronic monitoring

Market share was investigated in two ways: first, magistrates at 16 courts were asked to say for each offender sentenced during a ten-day survey which other disposals had been seriously considered; and second, court records were sampled from four courts in order to investigate whether those sentenced to curfew orders differed from those sentenced to other types of disposal.

The sentencing choices survey indicated that:

* curfew orders with electronic monitoring were seen as alternatives to custody and the higher end community penalties (community service orders and combination orders)

* magistrates used the sentence more often than it was proposed by probation officers in pre-sentence reports.

Analysis of case files revealed that:

* for a range of different offences, the use of curfew orders differed most significantly from the use of discharges and financial penalties

* differences between the use of electronic monitoring and custody or community sentences were generally not significant.

Costs of electronic monitoring

Using detailed information supplied by the two contractors (Geografix and Securicor Custodial Services), the costs of a national roll-out of curfew orders with electronic monitoring were modelled for a number of different scenarios, taking into account start-up and fixed running costs, as well as the costs based on the number of offenders tagged.

This model estimated:

* the average cost of a curfew order to be £1,900. This was less than the cost of a probation order (£2,300), but higher than for a community service order (£1,600)

* allowing for the fact that some curfew orders are made in conjunction with another community sentence raised the average cost to £2,700 per order. This is similar to the cost of six weeks in a local prison or remand centre, or eight weeks in a category C prison.

The future of electronic monitoring

Over the first two years of the trials of curfew orders with electronic monitoring, the technology has proved itself to be very reliable, and new, smaller tags (or personal identification devices - PIDs) were being introduced by both contractors from autumn 1997. The trials were initially expanded to cover a wider geographical area, then the length of the trials was extended and new courts given the authority to use the order. Starting in late 1997, a number of new areas will be phased into the ongoing trials: West Yorkshire, Cambridgeshire, Suffolk and the London boroughs within the Middlesex Probation Service area.

Finally, it should be noted that the reconvictions of those tagged in the first two years will be examined by the Home Office Research and Statistics Directorate once sufficient time has elapsed. The provisions of the 1997 Crime (Sentences) Act, which extended the use of electronic monitoring to deal with fine defaulters, persistent petty offenders and juveniles, will be piloted in Norfolk and Greater Manchester (starting in early 1998) and will also be evaluated. And, following the generally encouraging findings from the trials of curfew orders in England, the Scottish Office will begin piloting electronic monitoring as part of the new restriction of liberty order in the second half of 1998.

1 Introduction

Electronic monitoring was first introduced in England and Wales on a trial basis in 1989-90 as a condition of bail. These trials were not a great success in terms of take-up, partly because the monitoring equipment was unreliable, but also because of the way the new power was implemented – for example, bailees could be curfewed for up to 24 hours per day, and any time spent tagged was not taken into account in the event of a custodial sentence being imposed (see Mair and Nee, 1990).[1]

The Criminal Justice Act 1991 introduced the curfew order with electronic monitoring as a sentence in its own right. This was amended by the Criminal Justice and Public Order Act 1994 to allow the introduction of curfew orders with electronic monitoring on a trial basis to investigate the impact of the new sentence. The decision to introduce tagging as a sentence was influenced by a number of factors, including the apparent success with which it operated in the US and the desire for new, credible community sentences which would entail a clear restriction of liberty.

The trials began in July 1995 in the City of Manchester, the County of Norfolk and the Borough of Reading. The evaluation of the first year (Mair and Mortimer, 1996; Mortimer and Mair, 1997) concluded that the trials of curfew orders with electronic monitoring had been successful in a number of respects. In particular:

- the equipment had proved itself reliable

- the private sector contractors had carried out their duties to a high standard

- sentencers were pleased that breaches were detected almost immediately

- estimates of costs suggested that electronic monitoring was considerably cheaper than custody.

---

1   Under the current trials, offenders can be curfewed for two to twelve hours per day for up to six months.

However, the take-up of the sentence by magistrates and judges was disappointing, particularly in the early months of the trials, so that by the end of the first year only 83 offenders had been 'tagged'. Partly in response to the low take-up rate, two of the areas in which the order was available were expanded so that offenders living anywhere in Greater Manchester or anywhere in Berkshire were eligible, and the trials were extended to the end of March 1997. Subsequently, the sentence was made available to all courts in Berkshire (rather than just Reading) and Greater Manchester (rather than the City of Manchester alone), and the length of the trials was extended by a further year to March 1998. No changes were made during the first two years to the availability of the sentence in Norfolk, where all the courts could use it from the start.

Aims and objectives of the continuing trials

The trials were set up with three main formal objectives:

- to establish the technical and practical arrangements necessary to support the electronic monitoring of curfew orders

- to ascertain the likely cost and effectiveness of curfew orders in relation to other sentencing disposals

- to evaluate the scope for introducing electronic monitoring for curfew orders on a selective or national basis.

While the first year of the trials went part of the way towards meeting these objectives, the low numbers in the early months made it difficult to assess the feasibility and cost of a national roll-out of electronic monitoring. This report, which covers the second year of the trials (July 1996 to June 1997), is able to examine these questions in the light of the higher numbers achieved in the second year and using more detailed data. Further consideration is also given to the extent to which orders were successfully completed. Magistrates' views of the most appropriate offenders for curfew orders with electronic monitoring are also addressed, along with the differences between those sentenced to curfew orders compared to offenders sentenced to other disposals.

Methodology

This report is based on data derived from a number of different sources:

- centrally held information, supplemented by data from contractors, was used to provide overall figures on the number of curfew orders made, types of offence, and the proportion of orders completed or revoked

- a special 'sentencing choices' exercise, in which magistrates at a selection of courts involved in the trials were asked to record which other options they considered when passing sentence during a two week period. This information was used to discover whether the curfew order was seen as having a particular place in the sentencing framework and which other sentences it was replacing (i.e. where its "market share" comes from)

- samples of records from four magistrates' courts were examined to provide more detailed information about the characteristics of cases in which a curfew order was used, and how different these cases were from those which attracted other sentences

- a model of costs was developed using information held centrally and supplied by the contractors.

The focus of much of this report is on the adult magistrates' courts. This reflects the fact that, across the three trial areas, curfew orders were used less often at either the Crown or Youth Courts during the first year, and this pattern has continued in Year Two.

A reconviction study of those sentenced to curfew orders is planned. The data for this will become available during 1999. This will permit a standard two-year reconviction analysis of all those sentenced to a curfew order with electronic monitoring.

The use of electronic monitoring overseas

Electronic monitoring is being used in a number of other countries, including the US, Canada, Australia, Israel, Singapore and, closer to home, The Netherlands and Sweden. There has also been interest in electronic monitoring from other European countries and trials are currently being planned by the Scottish Office.

Electronic monitoring has been in operation in the United States since 1984, where it is used in a wide range of situations: as a bail condition; to enforce house arrest schemes; for early release from prison; and in combination with existing community-based programmes. It is used at county, state and federal levels. There has been no coherent national approach to tagging in the US, and much of the evidence from its use has been contradictory and/or inconclusive. Whitfield (1997) summarises some of the most important work in this field, and concludes that "good practice is not difficult to find but is still outweighed by poorly targeted, non-cost effective schemes which all too often increase criminal justice costs and prison populations by net widening".[2] In contrast to the US, the use of electronic monitoring is less widespread in Canada, though it has been used in British Columbia since 1987. It is currently available in four provinces but is not available at the federal level, mainly because the federal authorities are responsible for those offenders sentenced to two years or more in custody. There at least appears to be an attempt to conduct a coherent evaluation of the various schemes in Canada.[3]

Perhaps the most structured approach to using electronic monitoring is evident in Sweden (see Bishop, 1996a, 1996b and Somander 1995a, 1995b and 1996, as well as Whitfield, 1997). One interesting aspect there is that those targeted would otherwise have received a custodial sentence, and are placed under intensive supervision and monitoring by the probation service. They are also prohibited from taking alcohol or drugs for the duration of the electronic monitoring supervision, perhaps reflecting the fact that over half were convicted of drink-driving, which carries a mandatory custodial sentence in Sweden. There is a strict selection procedure for this programme, and Whitfield (1997) cites completion rates of 92 per cent (p.62). A similar success rate is cited for the programme in The Netherlands (Whitfield 1997, p.64), which targets those who would have received a prison sentence of 6–12 months, and others who may be selected to spend the last 1–6 months of a longer sentence being monitored electronically in the community.

---

2   Whitfield (1997), p.54.
3   The first part of this research – an evaluation of the electronic monitoring programme in British Columbia – has already been carried out (Bonta et al., 1997). This shows a 91 per cent completion rate, though the authors attribute this to the short duration of the programme and the relatively low-risk offenders selected (p.36).

Plan of the report

The next chapter gives details of the overall use of curfew orders, including the range of offences for which they were used, the criminal histories of offenders tagged and the extent to which they successfully completed the orders. The sentencing choices exercise and analysis of data derived from court records are described in Chapter 3, which draws some tentative conclusions about the market share of curfew orders with electronic monitoring. Chapter 4 discusses the costs of the trials and provides estimates for a national roll out. The final chapter brings together the results of the second year of the trials and discusses plans for expanding the use of curfew orders.

2 Offenders tagged during the second year

In this chapter we examine the number of curfew orders made over the course of the trials in each of the three areas, and compare this to the throughput of cases in the courts concerned. We look at the age and sex of offenders, their current and previous offending, and the outcomes of the orders.

The use of curfew orders was starting to increase by the end of the first year. The introduction of new courts gave fresh impetus to this, as can be seen from Figure 2.1, with orders being made at a far higher level than in the first year.[1]

Table 2.1 below shows the orders made in each of the three trial areas, broken down by the type of court.

Table 2.1 Curfew orders made by type of court in each area during the second year of the trials: July 1996 – June 1997

	Crown Court	Magistrates' Court (Adults)	Youth Court	Total
Greater Manchester	0	222	31	253
Norfolk	22	61	4	87
Berkshire	1	31	3	35
Total	23	314	38	375

---

[1] The dip in December's figures and peak in January's reflect the fact that courts are closed for the Christmas and New Year holidays.

Figure 2.1 New orders made by month

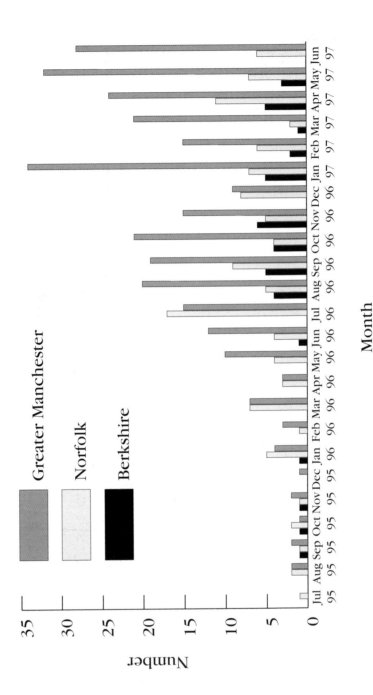

A total of 375 curfew orders were made by sentencers in the second year of the trials, more than four times as many as in the first 12 months, when 83 were made. Greater Manchester continues to dominate the trials, particularly Manchester City Magistrates' Court which alone accounted for 125 cases in the second year. (This is partly due to the high workload of the court – an issue which will be addressed later in the chapter.) Five times as many curfew orders were made in Greater Manchester as a whole in the second year as in Year One.

The biggest proportionate increase in the use of electronic monitoring was in Berkshire, although this sevenfold increase was from the extremely low base of five cases in Year One. The use of tagging in Norfolk continued to rise, with nearly three times as many orders as in the first year. This indication of the increasing acceptance of the new order by sentencers in Norfolk is especially noteworthy as, unlike the other two areas, no new courts were brought into the trials there.

Despite these big increases in the use of electronic monitoring in the adult magistrates' courts, the curfew order with electronic monitoring is a rarely used sentence when compared with other disposals. In the second year of the trials, over 300 curfew orders were imposed at the adult magistrates' courts, compared to 2,900 probation orders, 2,400 community service orders, 900 combination orders and 2,800 custodial sentences.[2]

The Crown and Youth courts still make very little use of the order. There has still been no Crown Court order from Manchester in the current trials, and only two (one in each year) from Reading. The Crown Court centres at Norwich and King's Lynn, however, made 22 orders in the second year, a quarter of the Norfolk total. It is not clear why there are such discrepancies in the use of the order between different Crown Court centres. Youth Court cases account for 10 per cent of all cases in the three trial areas.

Of the 375 offenders tagged in the second year, 346 (92%, slightly above the 90% figure in the first year) were male, and 29 (8%) were female. The ages of those curfewed ranged from 16 years to 77 years of age. The average age for all offenders was 26.4 years, almost identical to the figure for the first twelve months of the trials.

---

2   Home Office Crime and Criminal Justice Unit figures for the courts involved in the trials. Note that the data for curfew orders with electronic monitoring relate to the period July 1996 to June 1997, while data for other disposals are for January to December 1996. All of these figures have been rounded to the nearest hundred.

The average length for all orders made in the second year of the trials was 100 days (3.3 months, compared with 3.4 months in the first year). However, there was considerable variation between areas: Norfolk sentencers made the longest sentences, averaging 116 days (3.8 months), while the averages for Berkshire and Greater Manchester were 98 days (3.2 months) and 94 days (3.1 months) respectively.

Comparing curfew orders made with court throughput

In order to compare the take up of curfew orders fairly across different courts, the number of orders must be compared to caseloads. Table 2.2 shows the use of curfew orders during the second year of the trial as a rate per 1,000 adult offenders sentenced for the types of offences for which curfew orders were commonly used (i.e. all indictable offences, common assault, public order, driving whilst disqualified and driving with excess alcohol).[3] This figure was generated for all courts which were able to use the sentence from Summer 1996 and allowance was made for the fact that the sentence was available to some courts from July, whereas others (e.g. Newbury) introduced it some weeks later.[4]

---

3   Court activity data, covering all of 1996, were supplied by the Crime and Criminal Justice Unit, Home Office Research and Statistics Directorate.
4   Bolton, Rochdale and Salford were excluded on the grounds that curfew orders were only introduced there in 1997.

Table 2.2 Curfew orders – rate per 1,000 adult cases in magistrates' courts

Petty sessional division	No. of adult curfew orders made in second year	Curfew orders – rate per 1,000 adult cases sentenced
Bury	6	5.6
Leigh	8	11.3
Manchester	125	20.5
Oldham	10	5.0
Stockport	19	11.9
Tameside	31	24.8
Trafford	9	7.4
Wigan	8	5.3
all Greater Manchester (excluding Bolton, Salford and Rochdale	**216**	**13.9**
Central Norfolk (Swaffham and East Dereham	7	19.7
North Norfolk (Great Yarmouth and Cromer)	9	6.4
Norwich	33	16.8
South Norfolk (Thetford and Diss)	11	29.9
West Norfolk (King's Lynn and Fakenham	1	1.9
all Norfolk	**61**	**13.2**
Forest (Bracknell)	1	1.7
Maidenhead	11	25.0
Reading and Sonning	6	3.8
Slough	10	11.7
West Berkshire (Newbury)	3	4.9
Windsor	0	0
all Berkshire	**31**	**7.3**
all three areas	**308**	**12.6**

The figures in Table 2.2 should be treated with some caution as the court activity data used relate to January to December 1996, while the data on curfew orders cover the period July 1996 to June 1997. However, this is unlikely to affect seriously the results which show that differences within each of the three areas are greater than the differences between them. The greatest disparity occurs in Norfolk, where South Norfolk has the highest rate of orders made (29.9 per 1,000) while West Norfolk's rate is just 1.9 per 1,000. In Berkshire, Maidenhead has the highest rate of orders made (25.0 per 1,000) while Windsor has yet to make a single order. Only in Greater Manchester is there a smaller range between the most frequent users of curfew orders and those using them least, though even here the difference between Tameside (24.8 per 1,000) and Oldham (5.0 per 1,000) is striking.

Reasons for the discrepancies are not easy to find. King's Lynn (West Norfolk) saw the first offender tagged in the current trials. The offender in question repeatedly violated the order, leading to breach, revocation and resentencing to custody. This case attracted a great deal of adverse publicity from the national media and may well have been a factor in deterring local sentencers from using curfew orders. Given the small size of the workload at Maidenhead Magistrates' Court, there has been a relatively large number of curfew orders made. This may be related to the presence on the local bench of a former Chair of the Magistrates' Association who was involved in setting up the trials and was keen to see the new order properly tested.

Overall, the rate per 1,000 in Berkshire (7.3) was little more than half that of Greater Manchester (13.9) and Norfolk (13.2). Thus, the low number of orders made in Berkshire seems to be partly explained by a comparatively low caseload, but this alone is not sufficient to account for it. There have been suggestions from local sentencers and staff from Berkshire Probation Service that the size of the Personal Identification Device (PID, or tag) may have deterred sentencers, probation officers and particularly offenders from opting for electronic monitoring unless custody was the likely alternative. The gradual introduction of smaller PIDs from autumn of 1997, together with the removal of the need for consent to community sentences, may therefore result in a higher rate of use of curfew orders in Berkshire in the future.

Current offending

The main offence types which attracted curfew orders during the second year are summarised in Table 2.3.

Table 2.3 Main offences attracting curfew orders in Year Two

Main offence	No. of cases	Percentage
Theft and handling (including attempts)	104	28
Burglary (including attempts)	70	19
Driving whilst disqualified	47	13
TWOC / TDA (including allowing self to be carried)	31	8
Common assault (including ABH)	28	7
Driving with excess alcohol / while unfit	18	5
Criminal damage	14	4
Minor misdemeanours (including public order offences)	12	3
Assault on a police constable	11	3
Fraud and forgery (including deception)	10	3
Possession of drugs	8	2
Breach of a community sentence	4	1
Criminal attempts	3	1
Sexual offences	3	1
Minor motoring-related	2	1
Possession of an offensive weapon	2	1
Other, various	8	2
Total	375	100

N.B. Percentages do not add to 100 due to rounding.

As in the first year of the trials, the three most common offence groups for which curfew orders were used were theft and handling, burglary and driving whilst disqualified – between them these accounted for 59 per cent of all offenders tagged. Moreover, as the analysis of court records in Chapter 3 shows, this is not simply a reflection of the proportion of such cases coming to court. Taking without consent and taking and driving away have become associated with tagging in Greater Manchester, though the use of electronic monitoring for drugs offenders, which was relatively common in Norfolk in the first year of the trials, appears to have become much less frequent.

Previous offending

Table 2.4 below summarises the number of previous convictions of offenders sentenced during the second year of the trials.

Table 2.4 Number of previous convictions of offenders sentenced to curfew orders[5]

Number of previous convictions	Number of offenders	Percentage of offenders
0	45	12
1	39	11
2–4	83	22
5–9	77	21
10–19	95	26
20–29	25	7
30–39	5	1
40–64	2	1
Total	371	100

N.B. Information was not available on four offenders. Percentages do not total 100 due to rounding.

Forty-five (12%) of those tagged were first-time offenders, while one offender had 64 previous convictions. The average number of previous court appearances resulting in a conviction was 8.1. It is common for offenders to be convicted of more than one offence at each court appearance, so we also calculated the number of previous offences for each offender tagged. On average, offenders had been convicted of 20.3 offences. These figures for average numbers of previous convictions and average number of previous offences were slightly higher than for those tagged in the first year (7.7 and 17.5 respectively).

5   Criminal histories for tagged offenders were taken from the Offenders Index. This contains information on standard list offences only, which excludes many motoring offences. In particular, driving whilst disqualified has not always been included as a standard list offence, and this may therefore lead to a slight underestimate of previous offending.

Table 2.5 below summarises offenders' previous experiences of different sentencing disposals.

Table 2.5 Previous disposals received by offenders tagged in Year Two

Type of disposal	No. of offenders	Percentage of offenders
Absolute / conditional discharge	**223**	**60**
Fine	235	63
Compensation order	49	13
Any financial disposal	**243**	**65**
Supervision order	91	25
Attendance centre order	131	35
Probation order	137	37
Probation order with requirement	70	19
Community service order	176	47
Combination order	45	12
Any probation order	**162**	**44**
Any community sentence	**282**	**76**
Fully suspended sentence	50	13
Youth custody	129	35
Custody (adult)	119	32
Any unsuspended custody	**174**	**47**
No previous convictions	**45**	**12**
Total offenders	371	

N.B. Percentages total more than 100 as each offender may have experience of a number of different disposals. Information was not available on four further offenders.

Just under half (47%) of those sentenced to curfew orders during the second year of the trials had previously received an immediate custodial sentence (as opposed to a suspended one), slightly less than in the first year (54%).[6] Three-quarters had received some form of community sentence in the past. Of these, 44 per cent had been sentenced to probation orders, 47 per cent to community service orders and 12 per cent to combination orders. These figures are similar to those in the first year (52% probation, 45% community service and 12% combination orders). Two-thirds had previously received a financial penalty and six out of ten had been made the subject of absolute or conditional discharges.

6   For details of previous disposals in the first year of the trials, see Mair and Mortimer, pp 16–17.

Outcomes of orders

Table 2.6 below summarises the outcomes of orders made during the second year.

Table 2.6 Outcomes of curfew orders with electronic monitoring

Area	Orders completed	Orders revoked	Orders continuing	Total orders
Greater Manchester	196	52	5	253
Norfolk	76	6	5	87
Berkshire	28	6	1	35
Total	300	64	11	375

Excluding those orders still in force at the time of writing (October 1997), 82 per cent of orders made during the second year were successfully completed, which is an improvement on the 75 per cent figure for those tagged in the first year. This completion rate is better than for community service orders (71%) and the same as for probation orders (82%).[7] Judged on this criterion, electronic monitoring is clearly a worthwhile sentence. While it is true that community service orders and probation orders tend to last longer than a curfew order, it is also true that the enforcement of these orders (probation orders in particular) is more variable and sometimes less strictly applied than for curfew orders (see Ellis et al., 1996). Furthermore, the revocations include a small number which were terminated for reasons other than breach, such as the offender finding employment. The completion rates should therefore be taken as being, if anything, a slight underestimate.

The results in Table 2.6 are also noteworthy as they show an overall successful completion rate of 93 per cent for Norfolk compared with one in Greater Manchester of 79 per cent and Berkshire of 82 per cent. This is surprising given that, as mentioned earlier, Norfolk has the longest average sentence length of the three trial areas. Furthermore, the completion rate for the longest orders (from 5 to 6 months) in Norfolk is also very high, at 88 per cent (compared to 54% in Greater Manchester and 33% in Berkshire). As

---

7   Source: Probation Statistics, England and Wales 1996. The figure for successful probation order completions includes those replaced by a conditional discharge and those terminated early for good progress.

the focus of this report has been on the market share and costs of electronic monitoring it has not been possible to investigate the reasons for these differences. Whitfield (1997), has suggested that compliance may be affected by the nature of induction procedures, the way early (minor) breaches are responded to, and the quality of the relationship which develops between monitoring staff and the offender.[8] It may also be worth examining whether the targeting process at the pre-sentence report and sentencing stages differs between areas.

In all three areas there is a clear relationship between the length of the order and the likelihood of its being revoked. As Table 2.7 shows the shorter the order, the more likely it is to be completed without revocation.

Table 2.7 Curfew orders completed and revoked, by length of order

Length of order	No. of orders completed	No. of orders revoked	Percentage revoked
up to 1 month	12	0	0
>1 month – 2 months	74	4	5
>2 months – 3 months	118	23	16
>3 months – 4 months	53	14	21
>4 months – 5 months	14	7	33
>5 months – 6 months	29	16	36
All orders	300	64	18

N.B. This analysis excludes those orders still continuing at the time of writing (October 1997).

This is not unexpected: offenders who may find a curfew with electronic monitoring particularly difficult and who have received a relatively long sentence might decide at an early stage to withdraw their consent; those that continue with the order have a greater chance of accumulating sufficient absences to warrant breach action.

---

8   Whitfield (1997), pp. 91–92.

3 Identifying the market share of electronic monitoring

Findings from the evaluation of the first year of the trials of curfew orders with electronic monitoring suggested that the new sentence was viewed by sentencers and probation services as being towards the upper end of the community sentence band, and even as a possible alternative to a custodial sentence. During the second year evaluation, it was decided to examine this issue more closely. In particular, it was important to discover whether electronic monitoring had acquired a natural place in the sentencing framework and, if so, where that was. In other words, was it primarily used as an alternative to custodial sentences, an alternative to other community penalties (combination orders, community service or probation) or to lesser penalties such as fines or discharges? This examination of electronic monitoring's market share involved two separate but related exercises – a survey of magistrates' sentencing choices and an analysis of court records – the results of which are described below.

The sentencing decision: a survey of sentencing choices

Sixteen of the 20 courts in which curfew orders had been a sentencing option since summer 1996 took part in the sentencing choices exercise over a period of ten working days. Fifteen carried out the survey between May and July 1997, with the remaining court taking part in September. The remaining four courts were unable to take part within the tight timescale of the project. Courts where curfew orders were introduced more recently were excluded from this exercise on the grounds that it was too soon to expect them to have developed a clear view about where in the tariff the new order fitted.

Magistrates at participating courts were asked to complete one form for each offender sentenced during the course of the two weeks. As the focus was on the kinds of cases which could attract a community sentence, the following were excluded: cases where the offender pleaded guilty by letter; cases resulting solely in a bind-over; minor motoring and document offences; TV licence cases.[1] The form asked for details of the offender, the

---

1   As explained in Chapter 1, Youth and Crown Court cases were excluded from this exercise on the grounds that the vast majority of curfew orders have been made in the adult magistrates' courts.

main offence, the PSR proposal, and the sentence imposed. This purely factual information was sometimes supplied by court clerks, but magistrates were expected to provide the answer to the key question posed: "What other options were seriously considered by the bench in this case?".

A total of 801 valid forms were returned by the various courts. Table 3.1 shows these returns broken down by petty sessional area. Clearly some courts set out to provide details on all relevant cases, whereas others completed forms on only some of the potentially suitable ones. However, there is no reason to suppose the latter were deliberately selective or that this invalidated the results of this exercise.

Table 3.1 Number of cases from each Petty Sessional Area

Petty Sessional Division	No. of cases	Percentage
Bury	6	1
Leigh	7	1
Manchester	229	29
Oldham	105	13
Stockport	55	7
Tameside	37	5
Trafford	22	3
Wigan	129	16
Norwich	84	10
Great Yarmouth	33	4
West Norfolk	13	2
Central Norfolk	7	1
South Norfolk	22	3
Reading	20	2
Maidenhead	20	2
Newbury	12	1
Total	801	100

Ninety per cent of the cases on which sentencing choices information was obtained were dealt with by lay benches. Stipendiaries only sat at the courts in Manchester (where they dealt with 23% of the cases), Norwich (27%) and Great Yarmouth (13%). The number of offences for which offenders were sentenced ranged from one to 48, the average being between 2–3 offences.

The main offences were broken down as follows:

Table 3.2 Main offence types for all cases

Offence type	No. of cases	Percentage
Section 18 / Section 20 wounding / other serious violence	5	1
Assault on a police constable	12	1
Common assault / ABH	37	5
Sexual offences	3	0
Burglary (or attempt) in a dwelling	16	2
Burglary (or attempt) non–dwelling	19	2
Supplying drugs	4	1
Possession of drugs	28	4
Theft and handling	193	24
Fraud and forgery	16	2
Minor misdemeanours (e.g. breach of the peace, public order)	90	11
Criminal damage	39	5
TWOC/TDA	15	2
Driving whilst disqualified	56	7
Driving with excess alcohol	102	13
Failure to surrender to bail	2	0
Breach of community sentence	29	4
Other, various	127	16
Information not available	8	1
Total	801	100

N.B. Percentages do not total 100 due to rounding.

Information was also provided on whether a PSR was obtained and the main sentencing proposals such reports contained. The results are in Table 3.3.

Table 3.3 PSR proposals for all cases

PSR proposal	No. of cases	Percentage
Conditional discharge	27	4
Fine	10	1
Probation order	83	12
Probation order + requirements	58	9
Community service order	65	10
Combination order	27	4
Curfew order with electronic monitoring	10	1
Custody	2	0
No clear proposal	27	4
No PSR required	368	54
Total cases with PSR information[2]	677	100

N.B. Percentages do not add to 100 due to rounding.

Custody is almost never proposed in a PSR, but probation officers sometimes note in the report that there is no realistic alternative to it.

Table 3.3 indicates that probation officers writing PSRs only view curfew orders as the most suitable sentence in a small minority of cases. This is in line with the relatively low use of the order during the first year of the trials. However, it is worth noting that curfew orders were recommended as often as fines, and that there were no proposals in the survey for compensation orders or attendance centre orders (though the latter are only available for those aged 17–20). One explanation for the infrequent proposal of a curfew order could be that probation officers are more willing to propose community sentences they are familiar with and will exercise influence over if imposed.

The offences involved in the ten cases in which curfew orders were proposed were theft and handling (5 cases), driving whilst disqualified (2), burglary in a dwelling (1), burglary non-dwelling (1), and breach of a community sentence (1). The actual sentences made were five curfew orders, one curfew order combined with a probation order, two combination orders and two custodial sentences. Although the numbers are low, this does give some indication that, for the cases in this survey, PSR writers saw tagging as being a higher-end community sentence.

---

2   This table excludes 124 cases where there was no response to the relevant question. The base for Table 3.3 is therefore 677, as opposed to the overall total of 801 cases.

An estimate has been made of the annual number of orders expected to be made nationwide by magistrates' courts as follows. First we calculated the ratio of the number of curfew orders imposed in the second year of the trials to the number of persons sentenced for indictable offences at the magistrates' courts included in the trials. This proportion was then applied to the number of persons found guilty nationally.

The numbers arising from the Crown Court are more difficult to estimate. The take-up at Manchester Crown Court has been very low, while 22 orders have been imposed by Norwich Crown Court in the second year. It is not known whether judges' reluctance to use electronic monitoring will be overcome in future, or whether the take-up rate shown in the trials is a true indication of what can be expected.

The number of curfew orders imposed by Youth Courts during the trials does not provide a sure basis for projections. We have, however, estimated the number of these orders as being about ten per cent of those made by magistrates' courts.

We estimate that, at current take-up rates, for national roll-out about 6,000 orders or more would be imposed each year by magistrates' courts and Youth Courts, and in the order of 2,000 by the Crown Court. The results given here are therefore based where appropriate on a rough estimate of 8,000 orders per year.

Results – costs of national roll-out

The model that has been developed can provide cost estimates for chosen values of the following three main factors:

- average length served
- annual number of orders made
- number of field offices.

Our estimates of the probable values of these are based on the relatively small numbers of offenders arising during the trials. Of course, in the event of national roll-out, such factors as take-up rates and breach rates could be quite different.

Using information from the two contractors separately gives different estimates of overall costs. The proportion by which the estimates differ depends on the particular values of the three variable factors. The balance between the different elements of cost also differs slightly, for example, different proportions of staff costs can be included in the fixed charges and in the charges per offender. The results given here are based on a model which combines information from both contractors. The estimates are at current prices and exclude VAT. We have assumed that the two existing control centres will be in operation and will incur no start-up costs. If additional contractors were to be taken on then each would require a control centre, adding about £500,000 for each to the total first year cost. New field offices will be required for national roll-out. It has been assumed that their start-up costs will fall completely in the first year of operation.

Comparison of the components of the cost estimates

Figure 4.1, based on costs in the first year, shows a comparison of the components of costs. The greatest cost is the field office running cost, which is necessarily high even with a low volume of offenders tagged. The next greatest cost, at least at higher volumes, is the total running cost for all offenders, which depends directly on the number of offenders dealt with. At the top end of the range of numbers tagged the cost of any extra equipment required becomes more significant. The chart shows that the costs of breaches and changes of term are a small percentage of total costs.

Figure 4.1 Components of first year cost

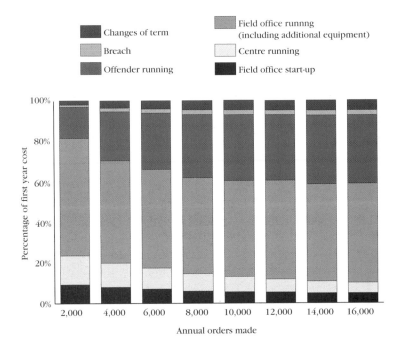

Each of the component costs shown in Figure 4.1 recurs annually except the start-up costs of field offices.

Total costs versus costs per order

The model shows the way in which costs would vary for different values of the three main factors. Not surprisingly the total cost would increase with increasing numbers of offenders, with more field offices and with a longer average length on curfew. However the cost per order shows a different pattern. For small numbers of offenders costs per order would be very high because the fixed costs are incurred for any number of offenders. Above an annual figure of about 6,000 offenders the cost per order varies little for a given average length of order.

Cost estimates

The model has been developed in order to be able to give cost estimates for a variety of possible uses of electronic monitoring. This section gives two estimates of the costs that would apply to the national extension of the current system. The first is based on an average or expected scenario, whilst the second is for an "upper limits" scenario. Results are given in Table 4.1. Should our expected number of annual orders prove to be an over-estimate, then the total cost would be less, while the cost per order would be slightly higher.

Table 4.1 Cost estimates for two scenarios

	Annual orders made	Number of field offices	Total first year cost	Cost per order
"Expected" scenario	8,000	30	£13,970,000	£1,750
"Upper limit" scenario	12,000	40	£22,500,000	£1,900

Comparison of costs with those for other sentences

Table 4.2 shows the average costs of probation orders and community service orders (taken from *Probation Statistics, England and Wales, 1996*) compared with the estimate for curfew orders with electronic monitoring. The curfew order cost is that for the "upper limit" case given above. The cost for the "average" case would be only slightly less.

Table 4.2 Average cost of different types of order, 1996/97 prices

Probation order	£2,200
Community service order	£1,700
Curfew order with electronic monitoring	£1,900

It can be seen that the cost of a curfew order is likely to be higher than that of a community service order, but rather less per order than probation. However, it must not be forgotten that additional costs will arise when probation and community service orders are imposed alongside a curfew order. The evidence from the second year of the trials in the Norfolk area (for which this information is most readily available) is that 24 per cent were given a probation order, 13 per cent community service and seven per cent a combination order, with the Crown Court much more likely to impose an additional order. (The numbers are too small to allow us to distinguish probation orders with added conditions.) Adding an element to allow for additional orders, the average cost of a curfew order would be about £2,700, rather more than a probation order.

It is difficult to compare the *overall* costs of curfew orders directly with custody. However, in the report of the first year of the trials the *monthly* costs of curfew orders and custody were compared. The same approach is adopted here.

Where curfew orders replace custody, that custody would ideally have been spent in a category C prison. However, any time spent on remand or waiting for a move to a category C establishment means that some or even all of a custodial sentence would be spent in a local prison or remand centre. The monthly cost (at 1996/97 prices) of custody is about £1,420 in a category C prison and £2,040 in a local prison or remand centre.[1] Comparing this with about £760 for a curfew order (including an element for additional community penalties), the cost of a curfew order is between a third and a half that of custody. Another way of expressing this is that the average cost of a curfew order would buy about eight weeks in a category C prison or six weeks in a local prison or remand centre.

---

1   Calculated from Prison Service Annual Report and Accounts 1994-95, uprated using the GDP deflator.

Overall costs and savings

The survey of sentencing choices described in Chapter 2, though based on small numbers, gives an indication of the sentences that might have been imposed had curfew orders not been available.

Diversion from custody

Custody was 'seriously considered' for nearly two-thirds of those on whom a curfew was imposed. Taking the estimate of 8,000 curfew orders and assuming that two-thirds of these replace sentences of three month's custody we estimate that more than 1,300 prison places would be saved on national roll-out. These places would be spread over prison establishments in England and Wales so it is not possible to say that the costs of one or more prisons would be saved in the short term. In the longer term, however, the potential savings, based crudely on the current costs of custody (realised as reductions in the prison building programme and in running costs), could be in the order of £20,000,000 to £30,000,000 a year. Balanced against the costs of electronic monitoring, this implies an overall saving of several million pounds a year. It should be remembered that we are extrapolating from a small sample, with the likely take-up of curfew orders by the Crown Court being in particular doubt. However, the savings would be increased substantially if, firstly, the use of curfew orders were to prove greater than that indicated by the trials, and if, secondly, electronic monitoring were to be made available for types of offenders not eligible at present. With good management and continued successful operation the first of these possibilities should be achievable, whilst the second is already being actively pursued.

Diversion from other sentences

The sentencing survey showed that community sentences, in particular community service orders, were also often considered in cases when a curfew order was chosen. As the costs of community sentences are similar to those estimated for curfew orders, a reduction in their market share would yield neither significant savings nor extra costs.

There is no firm evidence from the sentencing survey that other sentences would be significantly diverted to curfew orders. It is unlikely, therefore, that there would be a large loss of revenue from fines.

5 Conclusions

Use of curfew orders during the second year of the trials

Early in the second year of the trials of curfew orders with electronic monitoring, the availability of the sentence was extended to all of the courts in Berkshire and the majority of those in Greater Manchester. This, together with an increased acceptance of the order by sentencers, the probation services and other agencies involved in the trials, led to a much higher level of use of the order than during the first year.

A total of 375 curfew orders with electronic monitoring was made by sentencers in the three trial areas, more than four times as many as in the first year. Two-thirds of these were in Greater Manchester, a quarter in Norfolk, and one-tenth in Berkshire. The rate of use in the adult magistrates' courts was very similar in Greater Manchester and Norfolk – 13–14 per 1,000 cases, as opposed to seven per 1,000 in Berkshire. However, the rate of use varies much more within each area than it does between them.

The offences which most often attracted a curfew order during the second year of the trials were the same as in the first year: theft and handling, burglary and driving whilst disqualified. There was also a similar breakdown in terms of tagged offenders' previous convictions: almost half had previous experience of custodial sentences, and over three-quarters had previously been the subject of a community sentence.

Curfew orders in these trials continue to have a very high completion rate (82%), better than for community service orders, and identical to that for probation orders. The reasons for this are not clear, but may include effective targeting, a professional approach by the agencies involved and the relatively short overall length of curfew orders compared to other community sentences.

The market share of electronic monitoring

The analysis of magistrates' choice of disposals from the range of sentencing options suggested that curfew orders seemed to be used as a severe form of community penalty, and were effectively "in competition" with the higher end community sentences (community service and combination orders) and with custody. Analysis of a sample of court records, which was compared with those sentenced to curfew orders in the adult magistrates' courts, indicated that for most offences, the use of electronic monitoring differed significantly from the use of fines and compensation orders.

Costs of curfew orders

The costs of a national roll-out of curfew orders with electronic monitoring were modelled for a variety of different scenarios. The average cost per curfew order was estimated to be £1,900, slightly more than a community service order (£1,600), though less than a probation order (£2,300). However, allowing for the fact that some orders will be imposed in conjunction with another community sentence raised the average cost to £2,700. This is roughly equivalent to the cost of eight weeks custody in a Category C prison or six weeks in a local prison.

The future of electronic monitoring in Great Britain

The trials of curfew orders as a community sentence have been in place since July 1995, during which time the electronic monitoring technology has shown itself to be very reliable, and new, smaller tags were introduced in autumn 1997. The increase in the acceptance of electronic monitoring by sentencers, the probation services, social services departments and others, together with the consequent rise in the numbers of those tagged, have resulted in the expansion of the trials and the extension of the use of curfew orders.

With a scheduled start in late 1997, the use of curfew orders with electronic monitoring will be phased in progressively to a number of new areas: Geografix will be providing the service in the new areas of Cambridgeshire and Suffolk, while Securicor Custodial Services will be monitoring offenders in West Yorkshire and the eight London boroughs within the Middlesex Probation Service area.[1]

The 1997 Crime (Sentences) Act also made curfew orders with electronic monitoring available for three new groups of offenders: fine defaulters, persistent petty offenders and juveniles aged 10 to 15.[2] These new arrangements will be piloted in Greater Manchester and Norfolk, beginning in early 1998. Along with a range of other measures introduced by the legislation, the Crime (Sentences) Act also removed the requirement for

---

1   The eight boroughs are Enfield, Haringey, Barnet, Brent, Ealing, Harrow, Hounslow and Hillingdon.
2   Community Service Orders and disqualification from driving will also be available to sentencers dealing with fine defaulters and persistent petty offenders.

offenders to consent to a community sentence, including curfew orders with electronic monitoring. This took effect for offences committed on or after 1 October 1997. Finally, plans are under way in Scotland to pilot a new restriction of liberty order, to be monitored by electronic tagging. Trials of this order are scheduled to start in the second half of 1998.

References

Bishop, N. (1996a). *'Intensive Supervision with Electronic monitoring: a Swedish alternative to imprisonment'*. Vista, Vol. 1 No. 3 pp 23-30.

Bishop, N. (1996b). *'Intensive supervision with electronic monitoring'*. CEP Bulletin, June 1996. 'sHetegenbosch: CEP.

Bonta, J., Trytten, T., and Wallace-Capretta, S. (1997). *'Electronic Monitoring in British Columbia'*. Internal Preliminary Report. Ottawa: Solicitor General Canada.

Ellis, T., Hedderman, C. and Mortimer, E. (1996). *'Enforcing community sentences: supervisors' perspectives on ensuring compliance and dealing with breach'*. Home Office Research Study No.158. London: Home Office.

HM Prison Service (1996). *'Prison Service Annual Report and Accounts, April 1994 - March 1995'*. London: HMSO.

Home Office (1995). *'Availability of a new community sentence: electronic monitoring of curfew orders'*. Home Office Circular 36/1995. London: Home Office.

Home Office (1997). *'Probation Statistics: England and Wales 1996'*. London: Home Office.

Mair, G. and Nee, C. (1990). *'Electronic monitoring: the trials and their results'*. Home Office Research Study, No.120. London: HMSO.

Mair, G. and Mortimer, E. (1996). *'Curfew orders with electronic monitoring: an evaluation of the first twelve months of the trials in Greater Manchester, Norfolk and Berkshire, 1995-1996'*. Home Office Research Study No.163. London: Home Office.

Mortimer, E. and Mair, G. (1997). *'Curfew orders with electronic monitoring: the first twelve months'*. Home Office Research Findings No.51. London: Home Office.

Somander, L. (1995a). *'Intensive supervision with electronic monitoring: a description of the method with some preliminary results for the period August 1994 - February 1995'*. Norrköping: National Prison and Probation Administration.

Somander, L. (1995b). *'A year of intensive supervision with electronic monitoring: results for the period August 1994 - July 1995'*. Norrköping: National Prison and Probation Administration.

Somander, L. (1996). *'The second year of intensive supervision with electronic monitoring: results for the period 1 August 1995 - 28 February 1996'*. Norrköping: National Prison and Probation Administration.

Whitfield, D. (1997). *'Tackling the tag: the electronic monitoring of offenders'*. Winchester: Waterside Press.

Publications

List of research publications

A list of research reports for the last three years is provided below. A **full** list of publications is available on request from the Research and Statistics Directorate Information and Publications Group.

Home Office Research Studies (HORS)

151. **Drug misuse declared: results of the 1994 British Crime Survey.** Malcom Ramsay and Andrew Percy. 1996.

152. **An Evaluation of the Introduction and Operation of the Youth Court.** David O'Mahony and Kevin Haines. 1996.

153. **Fitting supervision to offenders: assessment and allocation decisions in the Probation Service.** Ros Burnett. 1996.

154. **Ethnic minorities: victimisation and racial harassment. Findings from the 1988 and 1992 British Crime Surveys.** Marian Fitzgerald and Chris Hale. 1996.

155. **PACE: a review of the literature. The first ten years.** David Brown. 1997.

156. **Automatic Conditional Release: the first two years.** Mike Maguire, Brigitte Perroud and Peter Raynor. 1996.

157. **Testing obscenity: an international comparison of laws and controls relating to obscene material.** Sharon Grace. 1996.

158. **Enforcing community sentences: supervisors' perspectives on ensuring compliance and dealing with breach.** Tom Ellis, Carol Hedderman and Ed Mortimer. 1996.

160. **Implementing crime prevention schemes in a multi-agency setting: aspects of process in the Safer Cities programme.** Mike Sutton. 1996.

161. **Reducing criminality among young people: a sample of relevant programmes in the United Kingdom.** David Utting. 1997.

162. **Imprisoned women and mothers.** Dianne Caddle and Debbie Crisp. 1996.

163. **Curfew orders with electronic monitoring: an evaluation of the first twelve months of the trials in Greater Manchester, Norfolk and Berkshire, 1995 – 1996.** George Mair and Ed Mortimer. 1996.

164. **Safer cities and domestic burglaries.** Paul Ekblom, Ho Law, Mike Sutton, with assistance from Paul Crisp and Richard Wiggins. 1996.

165. **Enforcing financial penalties.** Claire Whittaker and Alan Mackie. 1997.

166. **Assessing offenders' needs: assessment scales for the probation service.** Rosumund Aubrey and Michael Hough. 1997.

167. **Offenders on probation.** George Mair and Chris May. 1997.

168. **Managing courts effectively: The reasons for adjournments in magistrates' courts.** Claire Whittaker, Alan Mackie, Ruth Lewis and Nicola Ponikiewski. 1997.

169. **Addressing the literacy needs of offenders under probation supervision.** Gwynn Davis et al. 1997.

170. **Understanding the sentencing of women.** edited by Carol Hedderman and Lorraine Gelsthorpe. 1997.

171. **Changing offenders' attitudes and behaviour: what works?** Julie Vennard, Darren Sugg and Carol Hedderman 1997.

172. **Drug misuse declared in 1996: latest results from the British Crime Survey.** Malcolm Ramsay and Josephine Spiller. 1997.

No. 159 is not published yet.

Research Findings

30. **To scare straight or educate? The British experience of day visits to prison for young people.** Charles Lloyd. 1996.

31. **The ADT drug treatment programme at HMP Downview – a preliminary evaluation.** Elaine Player and Carol Martin. 1996.

32. **Wolds remand prison – an evaluation.** Keith Bottomley, Adrian James, Emma Clare and Alison Liebling. 1996.

33.   **Drug misuse declared: results of the 1994 British Crime Survey.**
        Malcolm Ramsay and Andrew Percy. 1996.

34.   **Crack cocaine and drugs-crime careers.** Howard Parker and Tim
        Bottomley. 1996.

35.   **Imprisonment for fine default.** David Moxon and Claire Whittaker.
        1996.

36.   **Fine impositions and enforcement following the Criminal Justice
        Act 1993.** Elizabeth Charman, Bryan Gibson, Terry Honess and Rod
        Morgan. 1996.

37.   **Victimisation in prisons.** Ian O'Donnell and Kimmett Edgar. 1996.

38.   **Mothers in prison.** Dianne Caddle and Debbie Crisp. 1997.

39.   **Ethnic minorities, victimisation and racial harassment.** Marian
        FitzGerald and Chris Hale. 1996.

40.   **Evaluating joint performance management between the police and
        the Crown Prosecution Service.** Andrew Hooke, Jim Knox and David
        Portas. 1996.

41.   **Public attitudes to drug-related crime.** Sharon Grace. 1996.

42.   **Domestic burglary schemes in the safer cities programme.** Paul
        Ekblom, Ho Law and Mike Sutton. 1996.

43.   **Pakistani women's experience of domestic violence in Great Britain.**
        Salma Choudry. 1996.

44.   **Witnesses with learning disabilities.** Andrew Sanders, Jane Creaton,
        Sophia Bird and Leanne Weber. 1997.

45.   **Does treating sex offenders reduce reoffending?** Carol Hedderman and
        Darren Sugg. 1996.

46.   **Re-education programmes for violent men – an evaluation.** Russell
        Dobash, Rebecca Emerson Dobash, Kate Cavanagh and Ruth Lewis. 1996.

47.   **Sentencing without a pre-sentence report.** Nigel Charles, Claire Whittaker
        and Caroline Ball. 1997.

48.   **Magistrates' views of the probation service.** Chris May. 1997.

49. **PACE ten years on: a review of the research.** David Brown. 1997.

50. **Persistent drug–misusing offenders.** Malcolm Ramsay. 1997.

51. **Curfew orders with electronic monitoring: The first twelve months.** Ed Mortimer and George Mair. 1997.

52. **Police cautioning in the 1990s.** Roger Evans and Rachel Ellis. 1997.

53. **A reconviction study of HMP Grendon Therapeutic Community.** Peter Marshall. 1997.

54. **Control in category c prisons.** Simon Marshall. 1997.

55. **The prevalence of convictions for sexual offending.** Peter Marshall. 1997.

56. **Drug misuse declared in 1996: key results from the British Crime Survey.** Malcolm Ramsay and Josephine Spiller. 1997.

57. **The 1996 International Crime Victimisation Survey.** Pat Mayhew and Phillip White. 1997.

58. **The sentencing of women: a section 95 publication.** Carol Hedderman and Lizanne Dowds. 1997.

Occasional Papers

Mental disorder in remand prisoners. Anthony Maden, Caecilia J. A. Taylor, Deborah Brooke and John Gunn. 1996.

An evaluation of prison work and training. Frances Simon and Claire Corbett. 1996.

The impact of the national lottery on the horse-race betting levy. Simon Field. 1996.

Evaluation of a Home Office initiative to help offenders into employment. Ken Roberts, Alana Barton, Julian Buchanan, and Barry Goldson. 1997.

Requests for Publications

Home Office Research Studies from 143 onwards, *Research and Planning Unit Papers, Research Findings and Research Bulletins* can be requested, **subject to availability**, from:

Research and Statistics Directorate
Information and Publications Group
Room 201, Home Office
50 Queen Anne's Gate
London SW1H 9AT
Telephone: 0171-273 2084
Fascimile: 0171-222 0211
Internet: http://www.open.gov.uk/home_off/rsd/rsdhome.htm
E-mail: rsd.ha apollo @ gtnet.gov.u.

Occasional Papers can be purchased from:
Home Office
Publications Unit
50 Queen Anne's Gate
London SW1H 9AT
Telephone: 0171 273 2302

Home Office Research Studies prior to 143 can be purchased from:

HMSO Publications Centre

(Mail, fax and telephone orders only)
PO Box 276, London SW8 5DT
Telephone orders: 0171-873 9090
General enquiries: 0171-873 0011
(queuing system in operation for both numbers)
Fax orders: 0171-873 8200

*And also from **HMSO Bookshops***